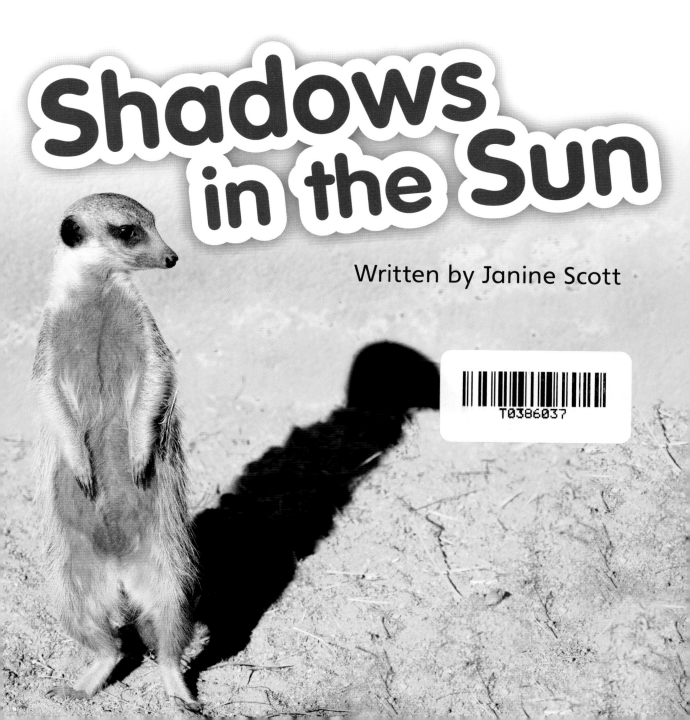

Shadows in the Sun

Written by Janine Scott

You can see shadows in the sun.

Look at my hand.

It makes a shadow
with fingers.

Look at this zebra.

It makes a shadow on the sand.

The shadow has a tail.

Look at this plant.

It makes a shadow on the sand.

The plant is bright but the shadow is dark.

Look at this plane.

It makes a shadow with wings.

Look at this meerkat.

It makes a shadow on the rock.

The shadow has a long nose.

Can you make a shadow?